D0576315

# FOSSIL FUELS
## Buried in the Earth

Amy S. Hansen

PowerKids
press

New York

Powering Our World

*To Christy Carmichael and other dedicated media specialists*

Published in 2010 by The Rosen Publishing Group, Inc.
29 East 21st Street, New York, NY 10010

First Edition

Editor: Amelie von Zumbusch
Book Design: Greg Tucker
Photo Researcher: Jessica Gerweck

Photo Credits: Cover David Hiser/Getty Images; pp. 5, 9, 11, 15, 22 Shutterstock.com; p. 7 © www.iStockphoto.com/Chad Anderson; p. 13 © Lou Jones/age fotostock; p. 17 © idreamstock/age fotostock; p. 19 © www.iStockphoto.com/Erlend Kvalsvik; p. 21 © www.iStockphoto.com/Rafa Irusta.

Library of Congress Cataloging-in-Publication Data

Hansen, Amy.
  Fossil fuels : buried in the Earth / Amy S. Hansen. — 1st ed.
      p. cm. — (Powering our world)
  Includes index.
  ISBN 978-1-4358-9325-2 (lib. bdg.) — ISBN 978-1-4358-9738-0 (pbk.) —
ISBN 978-1-4358-9739-7 (6-pack)
  1. Fossil fuels—Juvenile literature. 2. Pollution—Juvenile literature. I. Title.
TP318.3.H36 2010
  333.8'2—dc22
                                    2009019879

Manufactured in the United States of America

CPSIA Compliance Information: Batch #WW10PK: For Further Information contact Rosen Publishing, New York, New York at 1-800-237-9932

# Contents

What Are Fossil Fuels?                          4
Fuel from an Old Sea                            6
It Smells Like Rotten Eggs!                     8
A Black, Burning Rock                          10
Making Electricity at Power Plants             12
Going, Going, Gone                             14
Fossil Fuels Pollute                           16
Changing Our World                             18
What Is Next?                                  20
Fossil Fuels Timeline                          22
Glossary                                       23
Index                                          24
Web Sites                                      24

Long ago, people burned wood to stay warm. Today, we still sometimes burn wood, but we also use other **fuels**. We burn oil, natural gas, and coal. These are called fossil fuels. They are made from long-dead plants and animals. We burn these fuels to make heat and electricity. The **gasoline** that powers our cars, buses, trains, and airplanes is made from oil. In the United States, most of our **energy** comes from fossil fuels.

However, fossil fuels take millions of years to form. These fuels are **nonrenewable**. That means that once we use them, they are gone forever.

About 70 percent of the electricity used in the United States is made by burning fossil fuels in power plants, such as this one.

Every day, **pumps** pull up millions of gallons (l) of slimy, liquid oil. Most oil is underground, so people must pump it out to use it. Oil formed from small organisms, or living things, that lived in the seas. After these organisms died, their remains sank. Mud and sand buried them. This weight changed the remains into oil and natural gas.

For a long time, no one paid much attention to oil. Then, in 1908, Henry Ford started selling cars. As people began buying cars, they needed oil to make gasoline. Today, oil fuels about 450 million cars around the world.

Much of Earth's oil supply lies under the oceans. People build platforms, such as this one, from which they can drill for oil underneath the water.

# It Smells Like Rotten Eggs!

As oil did, natural gas formed millions of years ago from small organisms that lived in water. Natural gas is sometimes found alongside oil. Oil fields often have oil on the bottom and natural gas on top. People pump gas out of wells and **process** it. This produces both natural gas and other gases, such as propane, that can be used as fuel. Propane is often used in gas grills.

Natural gas cannot be seen or smelled. However, when **engineers** put natural gas into pipes, they add the smell of rotten eggs. This way, people can smell the gas if the pipes leak.

The burners on this stove use natural gas. Stoves often use natural gas. This fossil fuel is also often used to heat homes and power water heaters.

Coal is a hard, black rock. Unlike most rocks, though, coal burns. We burn it to make heat and electricity.

Coal started forming 300 million years ago, when Earth was wetter. Coal is made from the remains of plants that grew in the wet ground. When they died, these plants sank into the mud. They became spongy matter called peat. In time, rocks piled up over the peat. Their weight pressed on the peat. This dried the peat out and changed it into coal. We mine, or dig up, coal in many places in the United States and around the world.

After coal is mined, it must be taken to power plants. We use many methods, including trucks, trains, and boats, to move coal.

11

Electricity powers the lights in your school. Where does it come from? Wires connect the school to a power plant that makes electricity.

Most power plants burn coal, oil, or natural gas. The burning fuel heats up water. This turns the water into steam. The hot steam rises. As the steam rises, it turns a turbine, or giant wheel. The turbine turns a generator. This is the part of the power plant that actually makes electricity. Inside a generator, there are **magnets** and **coils** of wire. The generator spins the wires past the magnets. That movement makes electricity.

People who visit or work in power plants often have to wear special gear, such as hard hats, to keep themselves safe.

# Going, Going, Gone

Fossil fuels are running out. If you think about it, you can likely figure out why. Many people like having a car. Most cars run on gasoline. Once a car burns gasoline, the gasoline is gone. We cannot get it back again. Most people want electricity. Right now, much of our electricity is made from fossil fuels.

How long will fossil fuels last? That depends on how we use them. At the rate we are going, oil and natural gas may last for about 50 more years. Scientists think coal could last for about 200 more years. We must find other ways to power our world!

People today use a lot of electricity. For example, the lights and computers that we use in our homes, schools, and libraries all run on electricity.

# Fossil Fuels Pollute

When people burn fossil fuels, they send smoke into the air. The smoke is made of many gases. Some of the gases stay close to the ground and make it hard to breathe. Other gases make it into the **atmosphere**. This causes polluted rain, which hurts plants and animals.

Fossil fuels also pollute as they are taken out of the ground. Oil sometimes spills and makes a gooey mess. Coal dust blows away and poisons streams and rivers. The machines that dig up coal sometimes dig up forests as well. Pollution happens even when people are very careful.

When there is an oil spill, animals that live in the sea and along the coast often get covered in oil. Sadly, this can hurt or kill these animals.

The Sun sends energy to Earth. Much of this energy is **reflected** back into space. Some energy gets trapped by the atmosphere, though. This keeps Earth just warm enough for living things.

When we burn fossil fuels, we change that. Burning fossil fuels creates gases that end up in the atmosphere. The gases trap more of the Sun's energy inside Earth's atmosphere. That causes Earth to warm up quickly. This is called global warming. It causes ice and snow to melt faster. It also means some places have stronger storms and other places have fewer storms than before.

Global warming is causing the ice at Earth's poles to melt. This causes big problems for the animals, such as polar bears, that live at the poles.

Fossil fuels are useful. Burning them is an easy way to make electricity and heat. We also use fossil fuels to make plastics, nylon clothes, and other important things. However, these fuels pollute our world and they are running out.

Some scientists are finding new ways to burn fossil fuels in power plants. This would cause less pollution. It would also mean that we would need less of the fuels. This is a good first step. Other people are looking for different energy sources. If we can get energy from other places, we will need less energy from fossil fuels.

Wind power is among the energy sources that may replace fossil fuels. It uses turbines, such as these, to make electricity with the wind's energy.

# Fossil Fuels Timeline

| | |
|---|---|
| **300 million years ago** | Earth is warmer and wetter. Fossil fuels start forming. |
| **1765** | James Watt invents a new steam engine. It runs on coal and is used mostly to pump water out of mines at first. |
| **1858–1859** | North America's first oil wells are dug in Oil Springs, Ontario, and Titusville, Pennsylvania. |
| **1879** | Thomas Edison makes the first useful lightbulb. People soon start using lightbulbs and building power plants to make electricity. |
| **1908** | Henry Ford's **inexpensive** Model T hits the road. This is the first car that most people can buy. |
| **1970** | The American government passes the Clean Air Act. Power plants have to start cleaning up their smokestacks. New cars cannot pollute as much. |
| **1973** | Oil-producing countries in the Middle East stop selling oil to the United States. There is not enough gasoline to go around. Americans wait in long lines to buy gasoline. |
| **1997** | The **United Nations** agrees to try to slow global warming. The agreement, called the Kyoto Protocol, is signed in Kyoto, Japan. |

# Glossary

**atmosphere** (AT-muh-sfeer)  The gases around an object in space. On Earth this is air.

**coils** (KOYLS)  Curls.

**energy** (EH-nur-jee)  The power to work or to act.

**engineers** (en-juh-NEERZ)  Masters at planning and building engines, machines, roads, and bridges.

**fuels** (FYOOLZ)  Things used to make warmth or power.

**gasoline** (GA-suh-leen)  A fuel made from oil. Most cars run on gasoline.

**inexpensive** (in-ik-SPENT-siv)  Not costing very much.

**magnets** (mag-NETS)  Things that are pulled toward one another by a force called magnetism.

**nonrenewable** (non-ree-NOO-uh-bul)  Not able to be replaced once used.

**process** (PRAH-ses)  To treat or change something using a special series of steps.

**pumps** (PUMPS)  Things that remove liquid from one place and move it to another.

**reflected** (rih-FLEKT-ed)  Thrown back.

**United Nations** (yoo-NY-ted NAY-shunz)  A worldwide group formed to keep peace between nations.

# Index

**A**
airplanes, 4
animals, 4, 16
atmosphere, 16, 18

**B**
buses, 4

**C**
car(s), 4, 6, 14
coal, 4, 10, 12, 14, 16, 22
coils, 12

**E**
electricity, 4, 10, 12, 14,
    20, 22
energy, 4, 18, 20

engineers, 8

**G**
gasoline, 4, 6, 14, 22

**H**
heat, 4, 10, 20

**M**
magnets, 12
Model T, 22

**N**
natural gas, 4, 6, 8, 12, 14

**O**
oil, 4, 6, 8, 12, 14, 16, 22

**P**
people, 4, 6, 8, 14, 16, 20, 22
plants, 4, 10, 16
pumps, 6

**S**
space, 18

**T**
trains, 4

**U**
United Nations, 22
United States, 4, 10, 22

**W**
wood, 4

# Web Sites

Due to the changing nature of Internet links, PowerKids Press has developed an online list of Web sites related to the subject of this book. This site is updated regularly. Please use this link to access the list:
www.powerkidslinks.com/pow/fuel/